Flute and Piano
# THE WORLD'S GREAT CLASSICAL MUSIC

# The Romantic Flute

## 10 Favorite Pieces by the Masters

EDITED BY ELAINE SCHMIDT
Bryan Stanley, assistant editor

# CONTENTS

**Ludwig van Beethoven**          **Serenade in D Major**
                              5     Entrata
                              9     Final Movement

**Goerges Bizet**                21    **Entracte from *Carmen*, Act III**
                              24    **Minuet from *L'Arlésienne Suite No. 2***

**Fryderyk Chopin**              30    **Variations on a Theme by Rossini**

**Joannes Donjon**               37    **Pan**

**Gabriel Fauré**                40    **Sicilienne from *Pelléas et Mélisande***

**Friedrich Daniel Kuhlau**      50    **Divertissement No. 2**

**Emile Pessard**                45    **Andalouse**

**Camille Saint-Saëns**          62    **The Swan (Le Cygne) from *The Carnival of the Animals***

**Robert Schumann**                    **Three Romances**
                              66    I. Nicht schnell
                              70    II. Einfach, innig
                              75    III. Nicht schnell

On the Cover: Adolphe Mouron Cassandre, *Paris*

ISBN 978-0-634-04932-3

**HAL•LEONARD®**
**CORPORATION**
7777 W. BLUEMOUND RD. P.O. BOX 13819 MILWAUKEE, WI 53213

For all works contained herein:
Unauthorized copying, arranging, adapting, recording or public performance is an infringement of copyright.
Infringers are liable under the law.

Visit Hal Leonard Online at
www.halleonard.com

# FOREWORD

From the mannered music of the Classical era to the stormy symphonies of the late Romantics, the nineteenth century saw tremendous change in the world of concert music. The flute kept pace, changing dramatically as the decades passed. At the beginning of the nineteenth century the orchestra was growing in sound and size in the hands of Beethoven, and later Brahms and Schumann. Players of the gentle-voiced wooden flutes, which were quite popular among amateur musicians as the century began, had to struggle to be heard in the growing orchestras.

At first, a four-keyed instrument was considered quite modern at that time, but the Romantic composers' expanded use of harmonic color necessitated new key systems that allowed woodwind players to move freely throughout the chromatic scale in all octaves. In order to keep up with demands for greater sound, flute makers experimented with numerous materials for the construction of the instrument, including various woods, metals, glass, and even porcelain. In 1810 flutist/flute-maker Theobald Boehm built his first flute, attempting to create a key system that gave the player mastery over the chromatic scale. By the middle of the century, he had determined that flutes made of silver, and later, gold ones too, produced the best sound and were the easiest to play. It was a brilliant sound full of colors that could be heard clearly in all registers. Over the course of the next twenty years he developed the basic key system of rods, pillars, posts and springs. The new key system added technical possibilities, making the flute quite popular as a solo instrument. Boehm's key system is still in use on woodwind instruments today.

Playing nineteenth-century music allows flutists to explore the vast expressive possibilities of their instrument. As with music of any era, the best possible guide in learning these pieces can be found in listening to other music by the same composer, or a piece of the same era and style. Details, such as the way certain articulations are executed to create effects, become very important. Dynamics, air speed, embouchure, vibrato, and other elements that can influence the subtle shadings of the flute's sound are also part of the equation. It is in learning to use these musical tools that you create your own unique interpretations.

—Elaine Schmidt

# The Romantic Flute

## 10 Favorite Pieces by the Masters

**EDITED BY ELAINE SCHMIDT**
Bryan Stanley, assistant editor

## Flute Part

7777 W. BLUEMOUND RD. P.O. BOX 13819 MILWAUKEE, WI 53213

For all works contained herein:
Unauthorized copying, arranging, adapting, recording or public performance is an infringement of copyright.
Infringers are liable under the law.

Visit Hal Leonard Online at
www.halleonard.com

# FOREWORD

From the mannered music of the Classical era to the stormy symphonies of the late Romantics, the nineteenth century saw tremendous change in the world of concert music. The flute kept pace, changing dramatically as the decades passed. At the beginning of the nineteenth century the orchestra was growing in sound and size in the hands of Beethoven, and later Brahms and Schumann. Players of the gentle-voiced wooden flutes, which were quite popular among amateur musicians as the century began, had to struggle to be heard in the growing orchestras.

At first, a four-keyed instrument was considered quite modern at that time, but the Romantic composers' expanded use of harmonic color necessitated new key systems that allowed woodwind players to move freely throughout the chromatic scale in all octaves. In order to keep up with demands for greater sound, flute makers experimented with numerous materials for the construction of the instrument, including various woods, metals, glass, and even porcelain. In 1810 flutist/flute-maker Theobald Boehm built his first flute, attempting to create a key system that gave the player mastery over the chromatic scale. By the middle of the century, he had determined that flutes made of silver, and later, gold ones too, produced the best sound and were the easiest to play. It was a brilliant sound full of colors that could be heard clearly in all registers. Over the course of the next twenty years he developed the basic key system of rods, pillars, posts and springs. The new key system added technical possibilities, making the flute quite popular as a solo instrument. Boehm's key system is still in use on woodwind instruments today.

Playing nineteenth-century music allows flutists to explore the vast expressive possibilities of their instrument. As with music of any era, the best possible guide in learning these pieces can be found in listening to other music by the same composer, or a piece of the same era and style. Details, such as the way certain articulations are executed to create effects, become very important. Dynamics, air speed, embouchure, vibrato, and other elements that can influence the subtle shadings of the flute's sound are also part of the equation. It is in learning to use these musical tools that you create your own unique interpretations.

—Elaine Schmidt

# Flute Part
# CONTENTS

| | | |
|---|---|---|
| **Ludwig van Beethoven** | | **Serenade in D Major** |
| | 4 | Entrata |
| | 6 | Final Movement |
| | | |
| **Goerges Bizet** | 12 | **Entracte from *Carmen*, Act III** |
| | 10 | **Minuet from *L'Arlésienne Suite No. 2*** |
| | | |
| **Fryderyk Chopin** | 13 | **Variations on a Theme by Rossini** |
| | | |
| **Joannes Donjon** | 18 | **Pan** |
| | | |
| **Gabriel Fauré** | 16 | **Sicilienne from *Pelléas et Mélisande*** |
| | | |
| **Friedrich Daniel Kuhlau** | 19 | **Divertissement No. 2** |
| | | |
| **Emile Pessard** | 24 | **Andalouse** |
| | | |
| **Camille Saint-Saëns** | 26 | **The Swan (Le Cygne) from *The Carnival of the Animals*** |
| | | |
| **Robert Schumann** | 27 | **Three Romances** |
| | | I. Nicht schnell |
| | | II. Einfach, innig |
| | | III. Nicht schnell |

4

# Serenade in D Major
## Entrata

Ludwig van Beethoven
1770-1827
Op. 41

Copyright © 2002 by HAL LEONARD CORPORATION
International Copyright Secured   All Rights Reserved

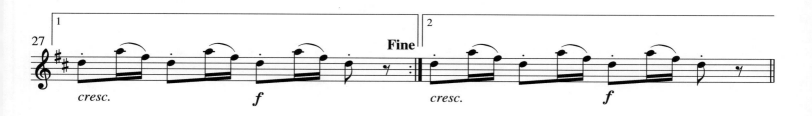

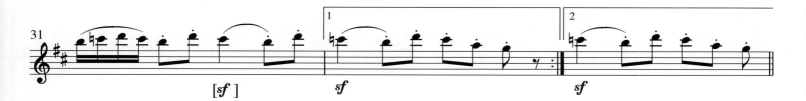

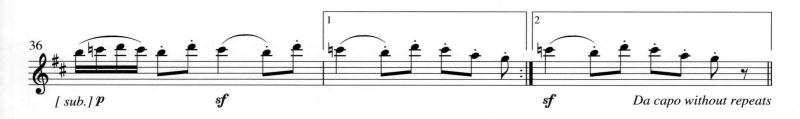

# Serenade in D Major
## Final Movement

Ludwig van Beethoven
1770-1827
Op. 41

**Allegro vivace e disinvolto**

Copyright © 2002 by HAL LEONARD CORPORATION
International Copyright Secured   All Rights Reserved

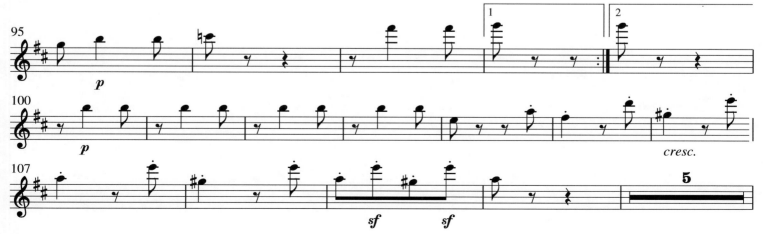

9

# Minuet
## from L'ARLÉSIENNE SUITE NO. 2

Georges Bizet
1838-1875

Copyright © 2002 by HAL LEONARD CORPORATION
International Copyright Secured   All Rights Reserved

# Entracte
## from CARMEN, ACT III

Georges Bizet
1838-1875

Copyright © 2002 by HAL LEONARD CORPORATION
International Copyright Secured    All Rights Reserved

# Variations
## on a theme by Rossini

Fryderyk Chopin
1810-1849
Posthumous

## Theme

## Variation I

Copyright © 2002 by HAL LEONARD CORPORATION
International Copyright Secured   All Rights Reserved

# Variation II

# Variation III

## Variation IV

**Allegro assai**

2nd time rit.

# Sicilienne
## from PELLÉAS ET MÉLISANDE

Gabriel Fauré
1845-1924
Op. 78

Copyright © 2002 by HAL LEONARD CORPORATION
International Copyright Secured    All Rights Reserved

# Pan
## Pastorale

Joannes Donjon
1839-1912

Copyright © 2002 by HAL LEONARD CORPORATION
International Copyright Secured    All Rights Reserved

# Divertissement No. 2

Friedrich Daniel Kuhlau
1786-1832

Copyright © 2002 by HAL LEONARD CORPORATION
International Copyright Secured   All Rights Reserved

22

23

# Andalouse

Emile Pessard
1843-1917
Op. 20

Copyright © 2002 by HAL LEONARD CORPORATION
International Copyright Secured    All Rights Reserved

*a tempo di più mosso*

*ff*

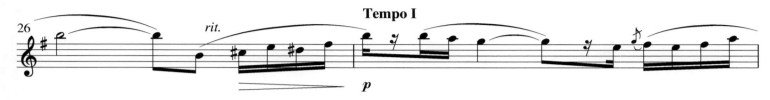

**Tempo I**

*rit.*

*p*

*p*

*rit.*

*f*

**Più lento**

*dolce*

*ten.* *rit.* *a tempo*

*ten.* *rit.* *ten.* *a tempo*

*f* 7

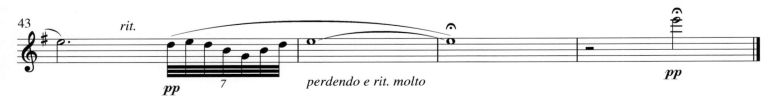

*rit.*

*pp* 7 *perdendo e rit. molto* *pp*

# The Swan
## (Le Cygne)
### from THE CARNIVAL OF THE ANIMALS

Camille Saint-Saëns
1835-1921

Copyright © 2002 by HAL LEONARD CORPORATION
International Copyright Secured   All Rights Reserved

# Three Romances

## I.

Robert Schumann
1810-1856
Op. 94

Copyright © 2002 by HAL LEONARD CORPORATION
International Copyright Secured    All Rights Reserved

55 *scherzando*

*p*       *fp*       *fp*

60

*pp*

66

*p*

72

*p*       *fp*

77

82

*pp*

## II.

**Einfach, innig** ♩ = 104

*p*

6

3

12

18

*3*

**Etwas lebhafter**

# III.

**CODA**

# ABOUT THE MUSIC

## LUDWIG VAN BEETHOVEN (1770-1827)
Serenade in D Major, Op. 41
    Entrata
    Final Movement

Beethoven's works straddle the Classical and Romantic eras. This serenade in particular, published in 1802 as a trio for flute, viola and piano, is Romantic in temperament. The popularity of the flute among amateur musicians at the time is evidenced by a letter Beethoven sent to his publisher telling him that perhaps someone should be found to transcribe some of his chamber pieces for flute. He wrote, "This could be useful to the amateur flutists who have already approached me about it and they would feast on it like a swarm of insects." It is thought that Franz Xavier Kleinheinz completed the transcription of the Serenade. The famously temperamental Beethoven had no interest in writing transcriptions himself, but he certainly had opinions on the transcription that was presented to him. He had his name placed on it, but in a letter dated 1803 Beethoven wrote about it: "The transcriptions are not by me but I have looked through them and in some places completely revised them. So I won't have it said that I did the transcriptions...and anyway I couldn't possibly find the time or patience for it." Included in this collection are the first and last movements.

## GEORGES BIZET (1838-1875)
Minuet from *L'Arlésienne Suite No. 2*
Entracte from *Carmen*, Act III

French composer Georges Bizet received his early musical training from his parents. He entered the Paris Conservatoire at age ten and completed his first symphony at age 17 while still a student. He went on to win the Prix de Rome and spent three years in Rome as a result. Despite the fact that we now regard him as one of the greatest of the French opera composers, his career was something of a struggle. Due to works left uncompleted and scores that were lost, it is not certain how many operas Bizet actually wrote.

*Carmen* was Bizet's last and greatest opera, but he never knew just how successful it would become. It was viewed as obscene at the time of its premiere, a condemnation that threw Bizet into a deep depression that adversely affected his health and hastened his death.

Bizet also provided music for a melodrama entitled *L'Arlésienne* (1872), which was intended to breathe life into the dying genre. Although the production was a failure, the music has survived in the form of two orchestral suites and in excerpted arrangements such as this.

## FRYDERYK CHOPIN (1810-1849)
Variations on a Theme by Rossini, Opus posthumous

The theme is drawn from "Non più mesta" in Rossini's 1817 opera *La Cenerentola* (Cinderella), the same theme which is also found in Act III in his earlier and most famous opera, *Il Barbiere di Siviglia* (The Barber of Seville).

This set of theme and variations are unique in Chopin's catalogue of works for several reasons. This is his only piece for a wind instrument, as the Polish piano virtuoso wrote principally for his own instrument. Written in 1824 and dedicated to Josef Cichocki during his first year of study at the Warsaw Conservatory, the variations give the flute the solo role and relegates the piano to a distinctly secondary role, unlike his other chamber music in which he treats the piano as an equal partner. These differences from his other works, combined with the fact that the piece does not bear any musical "fingerprints" of Chopin's characteristic style, lead some musicologists to doubt whether it is actually the work of the great pianist/composer.

## JOHANNES DONJON (1839-1912)
Pan

Frenchman Johannes Donjon was well known in his lifetime as a virtuoso flutist. He was a member of the Paris Opera orchestra, where he played beside two other famous flutists/composers, Henri Altes and Paul Taffanel. Donjon wrote light, romantic, salon music. He used his mastery of the instrument to create difficult sounding pieces that sit quite comfortably under the player's fingers.

## GABRIEL FAURÉ (1845-1924)
Sicilienne from *Pelléas et Mélisande*, Op. 78

French composer Gabriel Fauré was nearly fifty years old before he received any official recognition as a composer. He struggled to make ends meet for many years, working as a church musician and composing on the side, particularly during summer holidays. The tide turned in 1892 when he was appointed inspector of music of the state-funded conservatories. In 1896 he became Professor of Composition at the Paris Conservatoire and in 1905 was appointed director. He held this post until deafness forced him to retire in 1920. Today his song cycles, more than 50 songs, his Requiem and assorted piano pieces are considered masterworks.

In Fauré's Paris, a composer was not taken seriously until he had written symphonies or operas. Fauré looked for a suitable libretto for an opera for many years, writing incidental music for the theater in the interim. He wrote this sicilienne for Molière's play *Le bourgeois gentilhomme* in 1893 and later included it in the incidental music for Maurice Maeterlinck's play *Pelléas et Mélisande*, first heard in London in 1898. He also published a version of the piece for violin or cello and piano in 1898.

## FRIEDRICH KUHLAU (1786-1832)
Divertissement No. 2

German born Friedrich Kuhlau spent most of his life in Denmark and is considered one of the most important of the late Classical/early Romantic Danish composers. He was born near Hanover, where his father, grandfather and uncle were employed as oboists in military ensembles. In 1810, following the French annexation of Hamburg, Kuhlau fled to Denmark to avoid being drafted into Napoleon's army. Besides his international reputation as a concert pianist, Kuhlau's operas were quite popular in Denmark, although not performed outside the country. His song "King Christian Stood by the Lofty Mast" became one of Denmark's two national anthems.

Kuhlau's flute pieces are so well suited for the instrument that for a time it was mistakenly thought that he was a flutist himself. In fact, he took the advice of a flutist in the royal orchestra in order to write pieces that were truly idiomatic for the instrument.

## EMILLE PESSARD (1843-1917)
Andalouse, Op. 20

Pessard is remembered primarily as a Parisian composer of opera, although he also wrote orchestral and chamber music. It is not surprising that some of Pessard's chamber music included the flute. The instrument's colorful sound, combined with the virtuoso possibilities of the relatively new design of its key system, made it popular with the Impressionist school of composers in Paris. In Pessard's *Andalouse* one can hear a Spanish lilt, which reflects the Andalucia region of Spain from which the piece takes its name.

## CAMILLE SAINT-SAËNS (1835-1921)
The Swan (Le Cygne) from *The Carnival of the Animals*

French organist and composer Camille Saint-Saëns began writing music at the age of seven, undertaking public performances at age ten. Composer and piano virtuoso Franz Liszt referred to Saint-Saëns as the world's greatest organist. In addition to his work as an organist and as a teacher at the Ecole Niedermeyer, Saint-Saëns organized many concerts, revived public interest in music of the Baroque, and published writings on a variety of topics, including music, science and history.

"Le Cygne" (The Swan), originally written for cello and piano in 1886, is one of fourteen short pieces found in Saint-Saëns' *Le carnaval des animaux* (The Carnival of the Animals). *Le carnaval* was written on a holiday as something of a joke. With the exception of "Le Cygne," he did not allow performances of the pieces during his lifetime; reportedly fearing it would diminish his reputation as a serious composer. In the years since his death *Le carnaval* has become his most often performed work.

## ROBERT SCHUMANN (1810-1856)
Three Romances, Op. 94
     I. Nicht schnell
     II. Einfach, innig
     III. Nicht schnell

The son of a German bookseller, Robert Schumann studied music on the sly while leading his family to believe he was actually studying law. Once he was finally able to persuade them to allow his musical studies, his hands began to fail him. The story is told that he damaged his hands by using a mechanical contraption to strengthen his fingers, but his musical career was hardly over. In 1834 he founded the *Neue Zeitschrift für Musik*, a journal devoted to music. Schumann is one of the principal Romantic composers. He wrote over 300 Lieder, as well as important pieces for piano, orchestra and chamber ensembles.

*Three Romances*, written in 1849, was originally for accompanied oboe or violin, and has been appropriated by flutists, clarinetists, trumpeters and other instrumentalists since. Flutists play the pieces in the same keys in which they were written. Schumann approached these pieces with a vocal style of writing, creating melodies and moods reminiscent of his Lieder.

# Serenade in D Major

## Entrata

Ludwig van Beethoven
1770-1827
Op. 41

Copyright © 2002 by HAL LEONARD CORPORATION
International Copyright Secured    All Rights Reserved

8

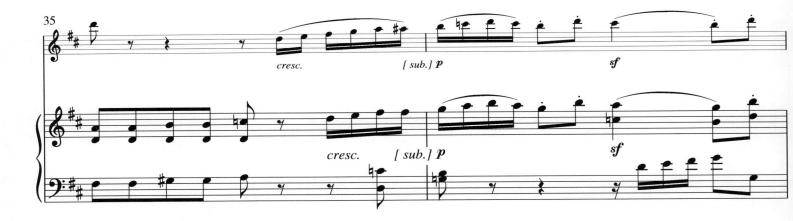

*Da capo without repeats*

# Serenade in D Major
## Final Movement

Ludwig van Beethoven
1770-1827
Op. 41

Copyright © 2002 by HAL LEONARD CORPORATION
International Copyright Secured    All Rights Reserved

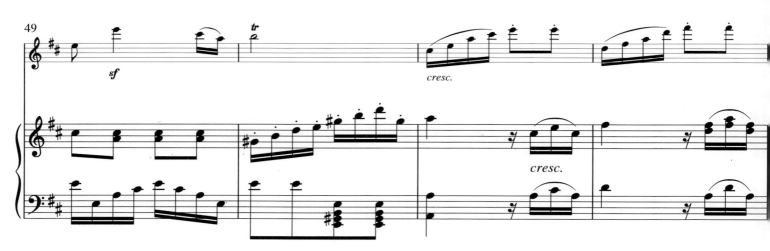

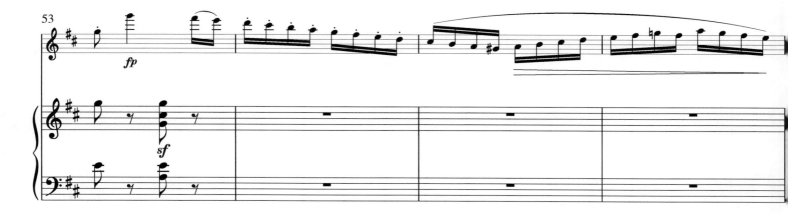

13

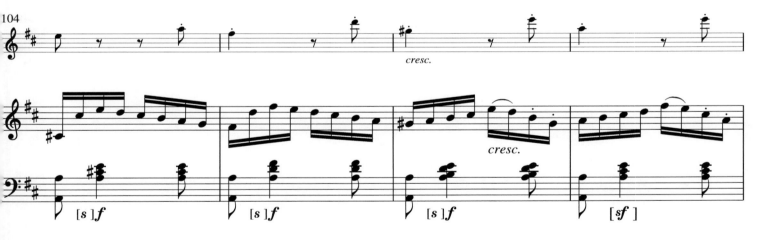

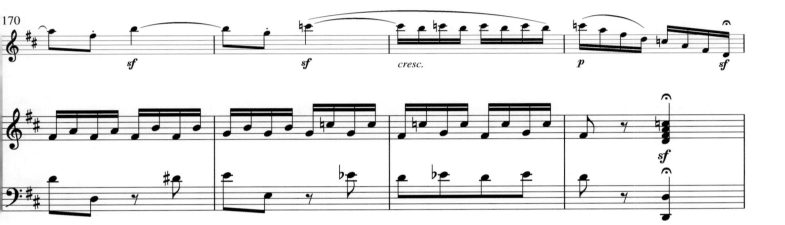

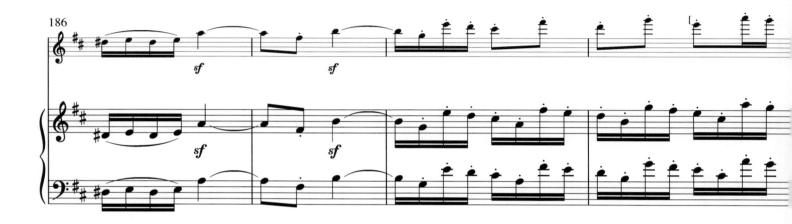

# Entracte
## from CARMEN, ACT III

Georges Bizet
1838-1875

Copyright © 2002 by HAL LEONARD CORPORATION
International Copyright Secured    All Rights Reserved

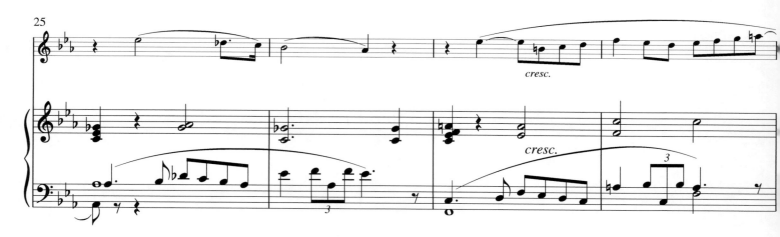

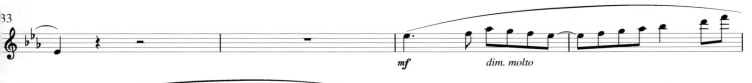

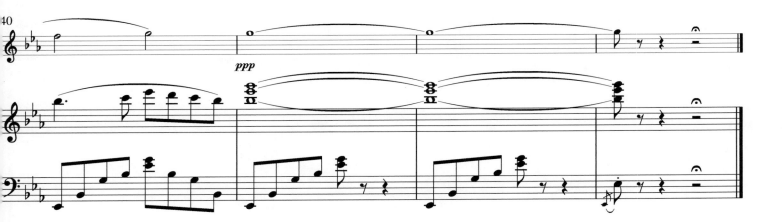

# Minuet
## from L'ARLÉSIENNE SUITE NO. 2

Georges Bizet
1838-1875

Copyright © 2002 by HAL LEONARD CORPORATION
International Copyright Secured    All Rights Reserved

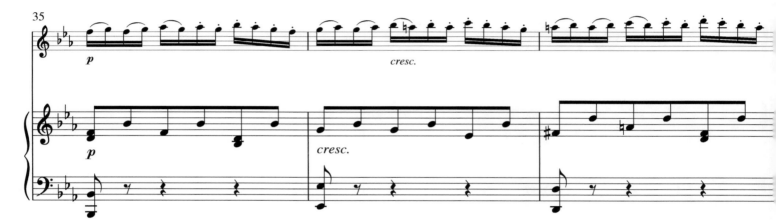

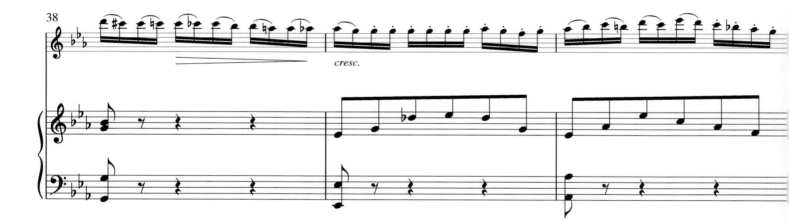

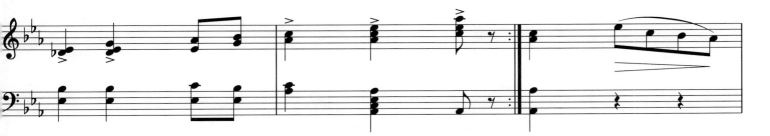

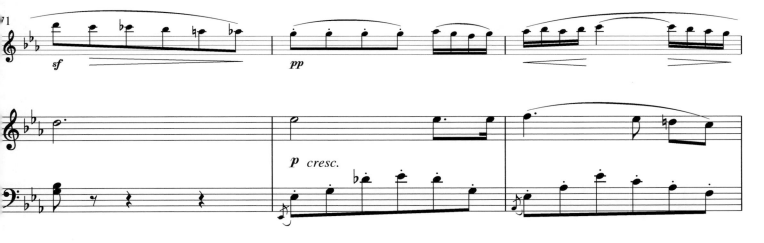

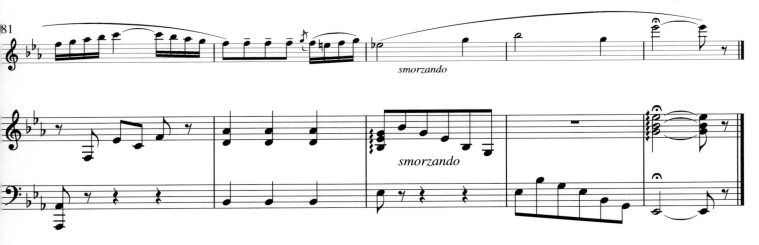

# Variations
## on a theme by Rossini

Fryderyk Chopin
1810-1849
Posthumous

**Theme**

Copyright © 2002 by HAL LEONARD CORPORATION
International Copyright Secured    All Rights Reserved

## Variation I

## Variation II

## Variation III

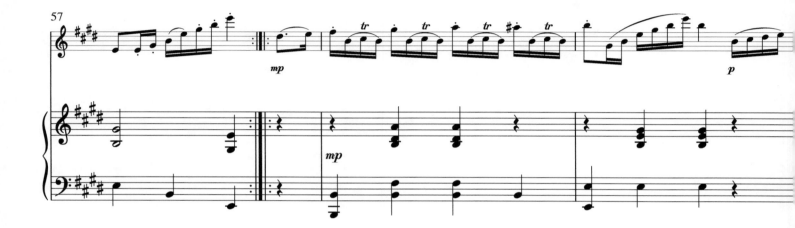

# Variation IV

# Pan
## Pastorale

Joannes Donjon
1839-1912

Copyright © 2002 by HAL LEONARD CORPORATION
International Copyright Secured   All Rights Reserved

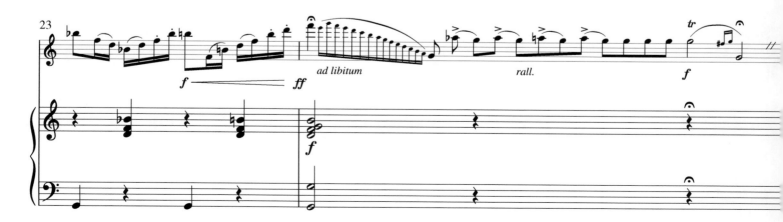

# Sicilienne
## from PELLÉAS ET MÉLISANDE

Gabriel Fauré
1845-1924
Op. 78

Copyright © 2002 by HAL LEONARD CORPORATION
International Copyright Secured   All Rights Reserved

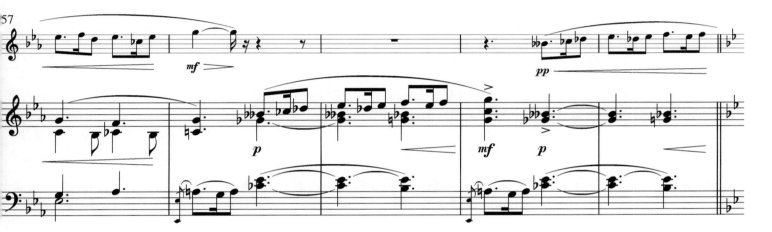

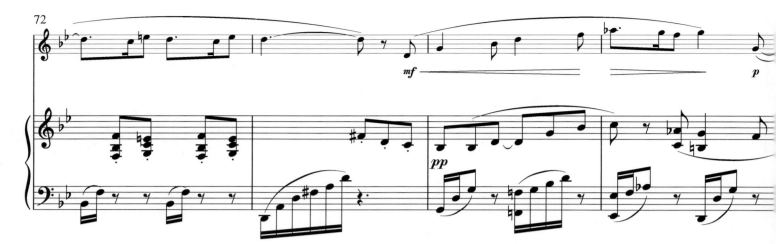

# Andalouse

Emile Pessard
1843-1917
Op. 20

Copyright © 2002 by HAL LEONARD CORPORATION
International Copyright Secured    All Rights Reserved

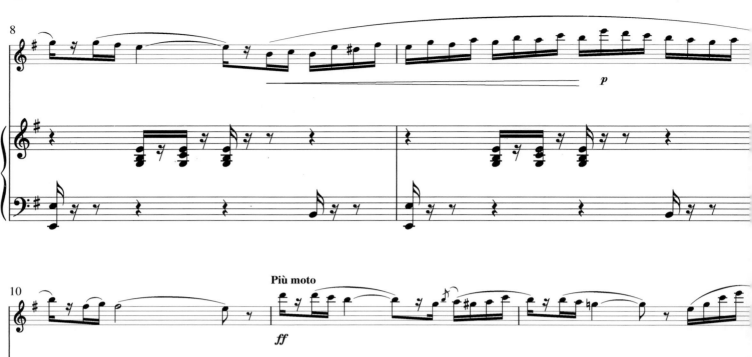

47

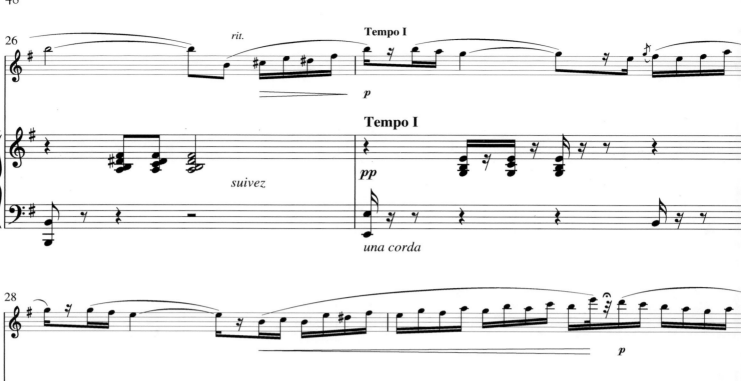

# Divertissement No. 2

Friedrich Daniel Kuhlau
1786-1832

Copyright © 2002 by HAL LEONARD CORPORATION
International Copyright Secured    All Rights Reserved

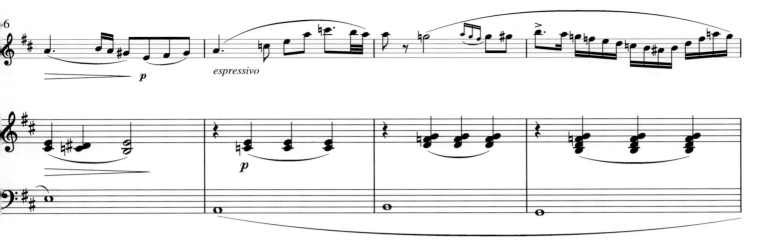

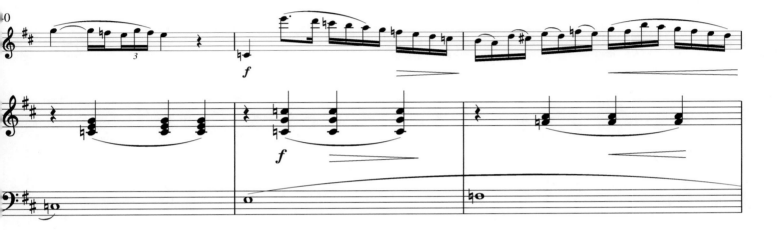

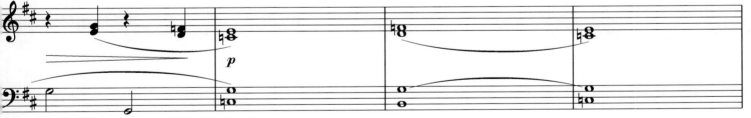

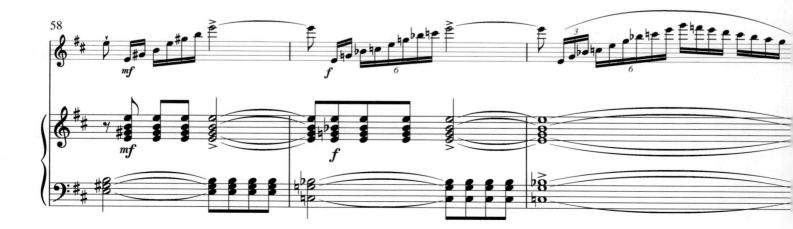

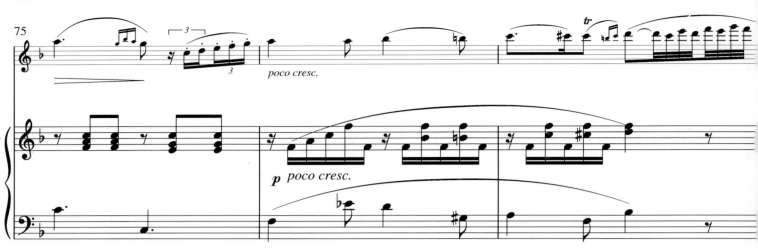

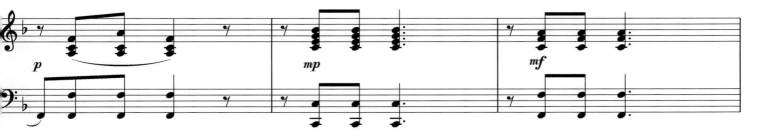

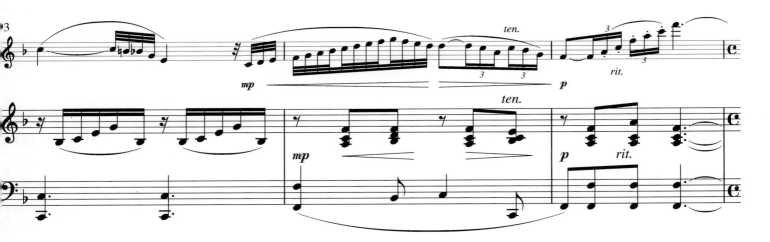

Tempo I

# The Swan
## (Le Cygne)
### from THE CARNIVAL OF THE ANIMALS

Camille Saint-Saëns
1835-1921

Copyright © 2002 by HAL LEONARD CORPORATION
International Copyright Secured   All Rights Reserved

# Three Romances

Robert Schumann
1810-1856
I.
Op. 94

Copyright © 2002 by HAL LEONARD CORPORATION
International Copyright Secured   All Rights Reserved

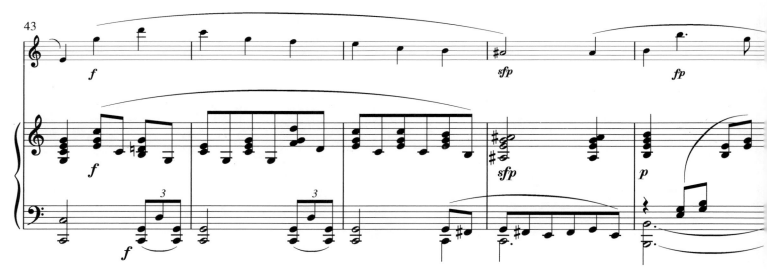

II.

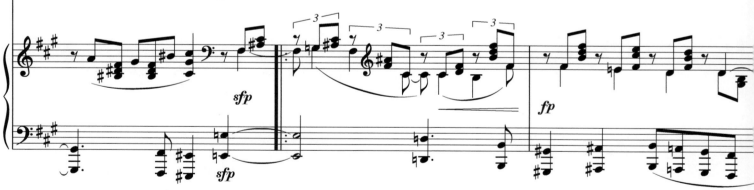

74

III.

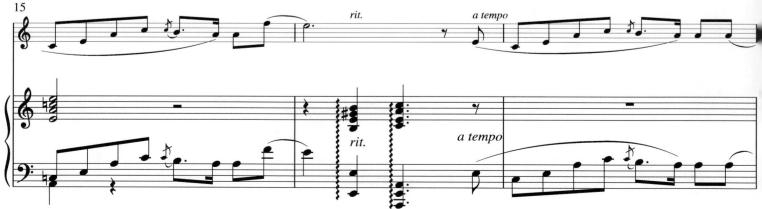

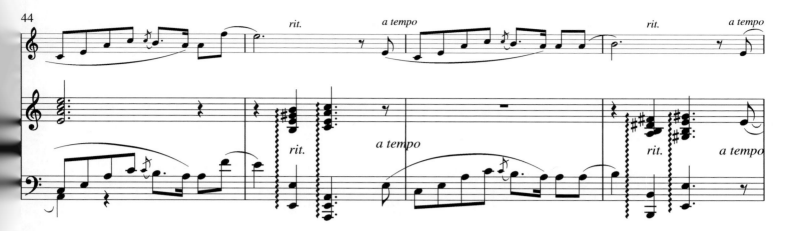

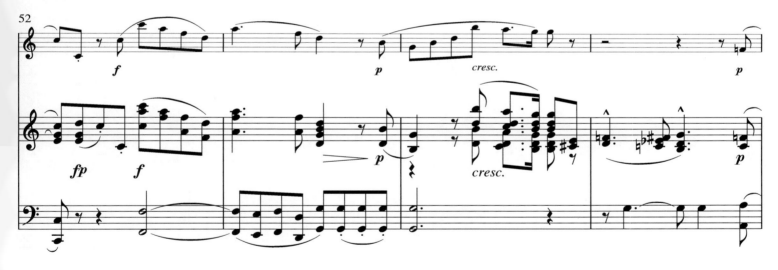

**CODA**

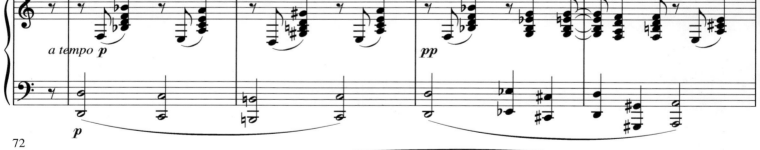